Summer at
Cove Lake

Written by Judy Nayer
Illustrated by Marni Backer

Dear Mom and Dad,

I'm here! I can't wait to see Cove Lake. Aunt Vee says she will take me there soon!

Love,
Rose

P.S. Do you miss me?

Dear Mom and Dad,

Today I went to Cove Lake! Aunt Vee let me use her fishing pole! I got two fish!

Love,
Rose

P.S. Do you miss me a lot or a little?

5

Dear Mom and Dad,

Today I went to Cove Lake again.

Aunt Vee and I sat on a big rock.
She said she sat on this rock
when she was little.

Love,
Rose

P.S. I hope you are having fun, too.

Dear Mom and Dad,

Today I found a frog. I saw it hop into the pond.

Aunt Vee says there are lots of frogs around here.

Love,

Rose

P.S. Do you like frogs?

Dear Mom and Dad,

Today we went swimming at Cove Lake.

Aunt Vee and I swam to a big raft. I jumped off the raft. I held my nose!

Love,
Rose

P.S. I hate to get water up my nose!

Dear Mom and Dad,

Today I went with Aunt Vee down the path past Cove Lake.

We picked blueberries.

On the way home I found a big pine cone. The pine cone is sticky.

Love,
Rose

P.S. I hope you like my pine cone.

Dear Mom and Dad,

Tonight Aunt Vee took me to Cove Lake.

We sat under the big moon.

The frogs said, "Rib-it." And the bugs lit up!

                       Love,
                       Rose

P.S. I'll be home soon.

Dear Mom and Dad,

Today is my last day at Cove Lake.
I will miss it a lot.

I will miss Aunt Vee, too.

Love,
Rose

P.S. I can't wait until next summer!